The Effects of a Choice Automobile Insurance Plan on Insurance Costs and Compensation

An Analysis Based on 1997 Data

Stephen J. Carroll

Allan F. Abrahamse

RAND
INSTITUTE FOR
CIVIL JUSTICE

Preface

Escalating auto insurance premiums have been a major public policy issue at the state level for the last three decades. *No-fault* auto insurance, born in the 1960s, was one response. It offered cost savings and speedier, more certain compensation to auto accident victims. But because it required that some claimants give up rights to seek compensation through the courts, many states found it an unappealing alternative. *Choice* auto insurance addresses this concern by giving drivers the option of selecting a somewhat modified version of their state's current auto insurance plan or a no-fault plan. In prior studies, the Institute for Civil Justice used data on auto insurance claims closed in 1987 and in 1992 to estimate how a choice plan would affect auto insurance costs in each state. This study uses more-recent data on claims closed in 1997 to update the results of those analyses. It uses exactly the same methods as were used in the earlier studies.

The Institute for Civil Justice has been conducting research on auto insurance issues since its inception in 1979. This study will be of interest to policymakers in each state concerned with insurance matters, to insurers, and to consumers.

For information about the Institute for Civil Justice, contact

Alan Charles, Director
Institute for Civil Justice
RAND
1700 Main Street, P.O. Box 2138
Santa Monica, CA 90407-2138
TEL: (310) 393-0411 x7803

Internet: alan_charles@rand.org

A profile of the ICJ, abstracts of its publications, and ordering information can also be found on RAND's home page on the World Wide Web at *http://www.rand.org*. The full text of many ICJ publications is available online through Westlaw at *http://www.westlaw.com*.

Contents

Figures

Summary

Overview

In 1999, bills that would establish a choice auto insurance plan in all states were introduced in the U.S. Senate (S. 837) and the U.S. House of Representatives (H.R. 1475). Under both bills, states would have the right to reject the choice plan and retain their current auto insurance plan. In earlier studies, we estimated the effects of a choice automobile insurance plan that embodies the basic principles of the plan being considered in Congress. The data we used in those studies described the compensation provided to representative samples of auto accident victims whose claims were closed in 1987 and in 1992. Recently, we obtained comparable data for a representative sample of auto accident victims whose claims were closed in 1997. Using these more recent data, we replicated our earlier analyses. This report presents updated estimates of the effects of the choice plan based on the 1997 data.

The Choice Plan

In the choice plan examined here, drivers are given a choice between a modified version of their state's current insurance system (MCS) and an absolute no-fault (ANF) plan. Each state's current rules govern the compensation of accident victims covered by MCS if they are injured by an uninsured driver or by a driver who elected MCS. Accident victims covered by MCS who are injured by a driver who elected ANF can recover for both economic and noneconomic losses, to the degree that that driver was responsible for the accident, under applicable state law (e.g., subject to the tort threshold in a current no-fault state). However, compensation would be paid to victims by their own insurer instead of the ANF driver's insurer. Accident victims covered by ANF are compensated for their economic losses by their own insurer, up to their policy limit. They neither recover for nor are liable to others for noneconomic losses. Any accident victim, regardless of insurance status, may claim against others involved in the accident, based on fault, for uncompensated economic loss.

We estimate the effects of a *basic* choice plan on auto insurance costs and compensation. The federal bills include provisions not reflected in this analysis. In particular, both the Senate and House bills would include commercial vehicles

Insurers' claims handling and defense costs would be reduced about one-sixth, on average. In addition, the choice plan would cut the costs of compensating uninsured motorists.

Sensitivity Analysis

We examined the sensitivity of our results to four fundamental assumptions that underlie the analysis—the fraction of drivers who go uninsured under the current system, the fraction of insured drivers under the current system who would switch to ANF under choice, the fraction of uninsured drivers under the current system who would purchase insurance under choice, and the frequency of very large loss cases. We varied one or another of the assumptions and repeated the entire analysis until we had systematically considered all reasonable possibilities in each state. In all, we developed 81 estimates of the effects of the choice plan on insured switchers' total auto insurance premiums in each state. For most states, the range of estimates is relatively small. Nothing in these estimates substantially affects our main findings of potential premium savings for ANF drivers.

Also, we used the same approach to develop 81 estimates for each state of the effects of the choice plan on total auto insurance premiums for drivers who elect to remain under the modified version of their state's current system. Here, too, the range of estimates is relatively small in most states. Nothing in these estimates poses a serious threat to our finding that insured drivers who elect their state's modified current system under choice would not be noticeably affected by the availability of ANF.

How the 1997 Results Compare to the 1987 and 1992 Results

Our updated estimates of the savings under the choice plan generally fall between estimates based on the 1987 data and those based on the 1992 data. In most states, our estimates of the savings that would accrue to drivers who opted for ANF based on the 1992 data were lower than the corresponding estimates we had obtained using the 1987 data. These patterns generally reversed themselves, though not entirely, between 1992 and 1997. That is, in most states, our estimate of the savings that would accrue to drivers who opted for ANF based on the 1997 data was greater than the corresponding estimate we had obtained using the 1992 data, though generally not as large as the estimate we had obtained using the 1987 data.

Acknowledgments

We owe thanks to many people for an enormous amount of help. We are greatly indebted to Jeffrey O'Connell (University of Virginia), who both brought the choice approach to automobile insurance to our attention and subsequently offered extremely valuable comments and suggestions on our analyses of the effects of a choice plan. We are also particularly indebted to RAND colleagues Lloyd Dixon, Deborah Hensler, Mark Peterson, Daniel Relles, and Robert Reville, who reviewed drafts of both this report and our earlier studies and provided numerous helpful comments. We have also benefited from comments and suggestions offered by the members of the ICJ's Board of Overseers who also reviewed our earlier studies.

We are particularly indebted to the Insurance Research Council (IRC). This analysis is based on data collected by the IRC. We also thank the Insurance Services Office, the National Association of Independent Insurers, and the National Association of Insurance Commissioners for data they provided us.

A great many people have contributed to our understanding of the workings of auto insurance systems. We cannot name every person who spent time with us; the list would be very long, and several of our conversations were on a nonattribution basis. We generally thank those public officials from many states, including judges, legislative staff, and staff from state insurance departments, who helped us understand the dimensions of the auto insurance policy debate. We also thank the many representatives of private organizations—consumer groups, insurance companies, and the plaintiffs' bar—who shared their perspectives and concerns with us. And we thank the people involved in the day-to-day operations of auto insurance systems—plaintiffs' attorneys, defendants' attorneys, and claims agents—who devoted many hours of their time to helping us understand how the auto insurance system works in practice.

Finally, we thank Elizabeth Giddens for helping us structure the report and Tracy Jenkins for typing the drafts.

Acronyms

ANF	Absolute No-Fault plan
BI	Bodily Injury
FR	Financial Responsibility
ICJ	Institute for Civil Justice
IRC	Insurance Research Council
ISO	Insurance Services Office
MP	Medical Payment
MCS	Modified Current System
NAIC	National Association of Insurance Commissioners
PIP	Personal Injury Protection
PPI	Personal Protection Insurance
TM	Tort Maintenance
UIM	Underinsured Motorist
UM	Uninsured Motorist
XEL	Excess Economic Loss

1. Introduction

Purposes and Scope of This Study

In earlier studies,[1] we estimated the effects of a choice automobile insurance plan on the costs of compensating auto accident victims. The data we used in those studies described the compensation provided to a representative sample of auto accident victims whose claims were closed in 1987 and in 1992. We have obtained comparable data for a representative sample of people whose claims were closed in 1997. Using these more recent data, we replicated the earlier analyses, using exactly the same methodology as we had used in the earlier studies.

The remainder of this section briefly reviews the choice auto insurance plan we examined, summarizes our research approach and the scope and limitations of this analysis, and presents our key findings.

The Choice Plan

Bills that would establish a choice plan in all states were introduced in 1999 in both the U.S. Senate (S. 837) and the U.S. House of Representatives (H.R. 1475).[2] The plan examined here embodies the basic concepts that underlie those plans. However, because of data limitations, we do not consider certain provisions of those plans. These are noted below.

In the choice plan examined here, auto insurance consumers are given a choice between a modified version of their state's current insurance system (MCS) and an absolute no-fault (ANF) plan. All drivers are required to purchase bodily injury (BI) coverage to at least their state's financial responsibility level. Drivers who opt for MCS are also required to purchase a new form of insurance, tort maintenance (TM), to at least that level, and, in the current no-fault states, the personal injury protection (PIP) coverage now required. Drivers who opt for ANF are required to purchase personal protection insurance (PPI) coverage to at

---

[1] Abrahamse and Carroll (1995), Abrahamse and Carroll (1997), and Carroll and Abrahamse (1998).

[2] Both the Senate and House versions of the plan would allow states to opt out of the federal plan and retain their current auto insurance plan.

least the state's financial responsibility level.[3] Drivers may purchase the same optional coverages now available in their state's current system: medical payments (MP), uninsured motorist (UM), underinsured motorist (UIM), and, in the add-on states, personal injury protection (PIP).

The rules of a state's current system govern the compensation available to victims covered by MCS if no other driver was at least partially responsible for the accident or if any other driver at least partially responsible for the accident was uninsured or had also elected MCS. At fault MCS-insured victims covered by first party, no-fault insurance would be compensated for their medical losses (under MP) or for all their economic losses (under PIP) by their own insurer. MCS-insured victims injured by an uninsured driver would be compensated for their economic and noneconomic losses by their own UM insurance, if they had purchased that coverage, to the degree the uninsured driver was at fault. MCS-insured victims injured by a driver who had also elected MCS would be compensated by that driver's BI insurance for their economic and noneconomic losses to the degree that driver was at fault.

MCS-insured victims injured by an ANF-insured driver in a tort state would seek compensation in fault for both economic and noneconomic losses from their own insurer under their TM coverage. In essence, TM insurance would operate as UM coverage does today. In the no-fault states, MCS-insured victims injured by an ANF-insured driver would be compensated for their economic loss by their own PIP coverage up to the policy limit. If their injuries surmounted the tort threshold, they would seek compensation in fault from their own insurer under their TM coverage for any economic loss not covered by their PIP insurance and for noneconomic losses.

An accident victim covered by MCS who was injured by an ANF-insured driver may seek compensation in tort from that driver for economic losses in excess of the victim's TM coverage. When claims for excess economic loss are pursued, a reasonable attorney's fee is recoverable, in addition to the excess economic loss.

In any state, victims who elected ANF are compensated by their PPI insurance for any economic losses resulting from an accident, including accidents involving drivers who elected their state's MCS, without regard for fault, to the PPI policy

---

[3]PPI covers the insured's economic losses (and funeral costs), regardless of fault, to the policy limits. It provides essentially the same coverage as the PIP insurance now required in current no-fault systems and available in many of the current tort states. We use the term personal protection insurance in reference to the coverage purchased by consumers who opt for ANF under choice to distinguish it from the personal injury protection coverage purchased by consumers who opt for the modified current system under choice in a no-fault state.

limit. Drivers electing ANF can never seek compensation for noneconomic losses.

Uninsured drivers injured in auto accidents proceed as under their state's current system if injured by either a driver who elected MCS or another uninsured driver. Uninsured drivers injured by an ANF-insured driver may seek compensation for their economic losses in excess of the mandated PPI limit, to the extent the ANF-insured driver was responsible for the accident.

Compensation for injured nondrivers—passengers, pedestrians, bicyclists, and so on—who have purchased auto insurance is governed by the rules relevant to their insurance, even though they were not driving when injured.[4] Compensation for injured nondrivers who have not purchased auto insurance is governed by the rules relevant to the insurance purchased by the driver who injured them.

Key Findings

Our results suggest that the choice plan could dramatically reduce the costs that insurers incur in compensating people injured in automobile accidents. Assuming that half of the currently insured drivers in each state were to switch to ANF under a choice plan and that insurance premiums are proportional to compensation costs, drivers in most states who opt for ANF could buy personal injury coverages for 57 percent less, on average, than what they pay for those coverages under their state's current auto insurance system. Because personal injury coverages account for a little less than half of total auto insurance premiums (property damage coverages account for just over half of auto insurance premiums), this reduction translates roughly into a 24 percent reduction in the average policyholder's total auto insurance premium. The estimated savings are not very sensitive to the fraction of drivers who elect ANF.

These estimates are overall averages: Individual policyholders would realize greater or smaller savings, depending on such risk factors as their driving record and where their car is garaged as well as on the personal injury and property damage coverages and policy limits they would purchase if ANF were not an option.

At the same time, the plan would have little effect on the costs insurers incur in compensating accident victims covered under the modified version of their state's current system. There is no reason to expect any significant change in the

---

[4]Motorists who choose either MCS or ANF bind their resident relatives to that choice.

insurance premiums charged policyholders who elect the modified version of their state's current system.

These savings result from reductions in the average amounts insurers pay out in compensation and transaction costs. In California, for example, we estimate that, on average, if half of the insured drivers in a state switched to ANF under choice, the amount paid to insured accident victims, including both those covered by ANF and those covered by MCS, for economic loss would be increased about 7 percent while the amount paid to them for noneconomic losses would be cut roughly in half. There are differences from one victim to another in how the compensation paid to them for economic loss under the choice plan would compare with the compensation they would each have received under the current system. Insurers' claims handling and defense costs on behalf of insured drivers would be reduced about 20 percent, on average. If half of the victims who were uninsured under the current system elect ANF when given the choice, the compensation paid to them would be reduced about 15 percent while the compensation paid to drivers who remain uninsured would be cut about 40 percent. The results for the other states are generally similar.

Scope and Limitations

Both the Senate and House versions of the choice plan would include commercial vehicles in the plan. However, because our data describe compensation paid under private passenger auto insurance coverages, we do not consider the effects of including commercial auto insurance in the plan.

Both bills would allow a victim to recover under tort when the injury was caused by a tortfeasor's alcohol or drug abuse, regardless of either party's choice. And drivers who elected the no-fault option under the choice plan would forfeit their no-fault benefits if they were injured while under the influence of alcohol or illegal drugs. Data limitations preclude inclusion of these provisions in the plan examined here.

The Senate and House bills would make PPI benefits secondary to other compensation sources, such as workers' compensation. Because our data do not indicate the availability of benefits from collateral sources, we do not consider the effects of these provisions in the analysis, and we assume that auto insurance is primary.

Finally, both bills would allow legally uninsured nondrivers to seek compensation under their state's current system from a driver who injured them regardless of that driver's insurance choice. Our data do not identify the insurance status of nondrivers injured in auto accidents. Accordingly, the plan examined here incorporates a provision that appeared in earlier versions of the federal bills. We assume that nondrivers injured in auto accidents are compensated under the option elected by the driver who injured them.

We assume that the distributions of accidents, injuries, and losses observed in the 1997 data for each state would have been the same in that state under the choice plan.

We estimate the costs of compensating the sample of victims in each state under either its current insurance system or the choice plan described above. The ratio of these estimates indicates the relative costs of compensating the same victims, for the same injuries and losses, under the two plans.[5] Because our results address relative costs, they do not consider whether auto insurance costs will rise or fall if a state adopts the choice plan. Rather, they show the difference between what would happen in that state if the current system is retained and what would occur instead if the choice plan were adopted.

We focus on how the choice plan affects auto insurers' compensation costs, including both the amounts insurers pay out in compensation and the transaction costs they incur in providing that compensation.[6] Because the choice plan has no effect on property damage coverages, we do not consider property damage in any of our estimates. To translate our estimates of the effects of the plan on compensation costs into estimates of the effects of the plan on insurance premiums, we assume that the many other factors (e.g., insurers' other expenses, profit margins, and investment income) that play a role in determining insurance premiums all vary in proportion to compensation costs. That is, we estimate savings on compensation costs and then estimate how total premiums would have to vary to maintain the existing ratio of total premiums to compensation costs.

We do not attempt to estimate the plan's effects on the costs of any particular coverage. Specifically, we compare the *average* amount insurers pay per insured driver under all coverages in the current system to the *average* amount paid under all coverages on behalf of drivers who choose either MCS or ANF under the choice plan.

---

[5]We include all accident victims in these calculations: insured and uninsured drivers, passengers, pedestrians, bicyclists, people injured in single-car accidents, and so on.

[6]Under the choice plan, victims may recover reasonable attorney's fees for a claim for excess economic loss. The attorney's fees paid by insurers as a result of such claims are included in our estimates.

For each state, we assume that the distribution of TM policy limits purchased by consumers who opt for MCS under choice would be the same as the distribution of BI policy limits purchased by consumers under the current system. The auto insurance compensation[7] for noneconomic loss available to victims injured by a driver insured under the current system in each state is limited to that driver's BI policy limits. The auto insurance compensation for noneconomic loss available to victims who elect MCS under choice in each state is limited to the victim's TM policy limits. Consequently, our assumption holds constant the average compensation for noneconomic loss available to consumers who elect MCS. If consumers who elect MCS under choice buy higher TM policy limits, on average, than the BI policy limits purchased under the current system, their savings would be lower and their access to compensation for noneconomic loss greater, on average, than our estimates. Conversely, if they buy lower TM policy limits, on average, than the BI policy limits purchased under the current system, their savings would be greater and their access to compensation for noneconomic loss less, on average, than our estimates.

Furthermore, because our focus is on the financial implications of the choice plan, we do not consider the degree to which victims derive satisfaction from being compensated under an insurance policy purchased by the driver who injured them. Nor do we consider the satisfaction that consumers who value access to compensation for noneconomic loss derive from being able to determine for themselves the limits on what they can obtain if injured by another driver in an auto accident rather than facing the uncertainty of the policy limit purchased by that driver.

The current system in most states encourages victims to exaggerate their medical costs as a means of leveraging larger settlements from auto insurers.[8] The ANF option would eliminate this incentive for excess claims. To the extent that the distributions of claimed economic losses reflect excess claiming in response to the current system, drivers who elect ANF under choice would submit fewer, smaller claims than we assume. The choice plan might thus result in greater savings than those reported here.[9]

---

[7]Because our concern is for the effects of the choice plan on private passenger auto insurance costs, we address only the effects of the plan on the costs incurred by auto insurers in covering private passenger vehicles. People injured in auto accidents may obtain compensation for noneconomic loss from other forms of insurance such as personal umbrella or business liability coverages.

[8]See, for example, Carroll et al. (1995) or Insurance Research Council (1996).

[9]Some victims who could not have recovered from any auto insurer under the tort system (e.g., a totally at-fault driver who had not purchased the optional no-fault insurance, MP or PIP, available in the tort states) will be compensated if they elected ANF under the choice plan. These claims are included in this analysis.

Hawaii and New Jersey made significant changes to their auto insurance systems after 1997. Our data do not provide a basis for estimating the effects of a choice plan in those states; we excluded them from this analysis.

Pennsylvania offers consumers a choice plan under which they could elect either tort or a verbal threshold no-fault plan.[10] We performed separate analyses for the effects of each plan. In the subsequent tables, the effects of the plan on Pennsylvania drivers who elected tort, labeled Penn (tort), are included in the results for the tort states; the effects of the plan on Pennsylvania drivers who elected no-fault, labeled Penn (nof), are included in the results for the no-fault states.

Organization of the Discussion

The remainder of this discussion is organized as follows. In Section 2, we describe our research approach, including the data and the methods we used to estimate compensation costs under either the current system or the choice plan in each state and the relative savings under the choice plan compared to the current system. Because we used exactly the same methods as we had used in our earlier studies, much of Section 2 is taken verbatim from our earlier reports. Section 3 presents our findings and describes the sensitivity analyses we conducted. Finally, Section 4 contains our conclusions. The Appendix presents the technical details of certain calculations.

---

[10]Under a verbal threshold auto insurance plan, injured parties may seek compensation for noneconomic loss if they have suffered certain injuries specified in the law. Examples of the language found in the various verbal thresholds now in use are "death" (all), "significant and permanent loss of an important bodily function" (Florida), "permanent serious disfigurement" (Michigan and Pennsylvania), "dismemberment" (New Jersey), and "permanent consequential limitation of use of a body function or system" (New York).

2. Research Approach

We estimate the relative cost effects of the choice plan in each state in three steps: (1) We estimate the average cost of compensating accident victims under the current system and the corresponding "break-even premium"—the premium an insurance company must charge to cover exactly what it pays in claims and the associated transaction costs; (2) we estimate the average cost of compensating accident victims on behalf of drivers who elect either MCS or ANF under the choice system and the break-even premiums for each class of driver; and (3) we calculate relative savings under choice as the percentage difference between the break-even premium under choice for drivers who elect either option and the break-even premium under the current system.

We describe our data and methods below. The 1997 data were collected according to the same protocols and, from the perspective of this study, using the same instruments[1] as were the 1992 data. We used the same methods as we used in our earlier studies. Accordingly, the following description of the data and methodology used in this study is largely reproduced from our earlier reports.

Data

The analysis relies on data from four sources: closed claim surveys conducted by the Insurance Research Council (IRC);[2] special tabulations compiled at our request by the Insurance Services Office (ISO); and National Association of Insurance Commissioners (NAIC) reports on auto insurance premiums by type of coverage.[3]

The closed claim surveys obtained detailed information on a national representative sample of auto accident injury claims closed with payment during 1997 under each of the principal auto injury coverages—BI, MP, UM, UIM, and PIP.[4] The data detail each victim's accident and resulting injuries and losses, as well as the compensation each victim obtained from auto insurance. The data

---

[1]None of the items that obtained the information used in this study was changed between 1992 and 1997.

[2]Insurance Research Council (1999b) provides a detailed description of the closed claim surveys.

[3]National Association of Insurance Commissioners (1999).

[4]These are the most recent available data that describe the outcomes of a national sample of individual claims.

were collected by 40 insurance companies that, together, accounted for about 67 percent of private passenger automobile insurance by premium volume at the time the data were collected. In each state and for each coverage, the survey represents a simple random sample of all claims closed in that state by the participating companies.[5]

We used the ISO data to estimate insurers' transaction costs,[6] including both allocated loss-adjustment costs—legal fees and related expenses incurred on behalf of and directly attributed to a specific claim—and unallocated, or general claims processing, costs, for each line of private passenger auto insurance.[7] We estimate insurers' allocated loss-adjustment expenses as 1 percent of MP compensation paid, 1 percent of PIP compensation paid, 10 percent of BI compensation paid, and 8 percent of UM or UIM compensation paid. We estimate insurers' unallocated loss-adjustment expenses as 8 percent of paid compensation for each type of coverage. The plan provides that anyone who seeks compensation for economic loss in excess of the mandated PIP limit can recover attorneys' fees; we assume claimants' attorneys' fees average 31 percent.[8]

The NAIC reports private passenger automobile insurance premiums by state and coverage for 1997, the most recent year for which these data are available.

Estimating Compensation Costs Under the Current System

To estimate compensation costs under the current system, we identified the sources of auto insurance compensation that would be available to accident victims, depending on the type of insurance that they and others purchase. We then estimated the average amount of compensation that would be paid by each source, and the associated transaction costs, to a representative sample of auto

---

[5]The sampling fraction differs from state to state. We estimate the effects of the choice plan in each state, using the data for that state. To obtain an estimate of the nationwide effects of the plan, we combine the results across states, weighting the result for each state by the product of the sampling fraction for that state and the number of auto insurance policies sold in that state in 1997. We obtained the data on the number of policies written in each state from National Association of Insurance Commissioners (1999).

[6]Carroll et al. (1991), Appendix D, describes the data and methods used to estimate insurers' transaction costs.

[7]We do not include victims' legal costs, the value of victims' time, or the costs the courts incur in handling litigated claims. Those costs do not affect insurers' costs and hence do not affect auto insurance premiums.

[8]We do not suggest that attorneys will necessarily charge accident victims a 31 percent contingency fee to represent them in seeking compensation for economic loss in excess of policy limits. However, plaintiff attorneys' fees now average about 31 percent of victims' recovery. If plaintiff attorneys' compensation in the current system is reasonable and fair, their fees—whether charged on an hourly basis, as a contingency, or by some other system—would presumably be approximately as large, relative to the victims' recovery, under the choice plan.

accident victims from each state. Finally, we assumed a distribution of insurance purchase decisions (i.e., the coverages and limits purchased) and computed the expected compensation paid to the average accident victim, given that distribution. The result is an estimate of the compensation costs, including transaction costs, incurred under each state's current system for the assumed distribution of insurance purchase decisions.

In the sensitivity analyses (discussed in Section 3), we examine the extent to which our estimates vary with alternative compensation estimates or assumed distributions of insurance purchase decisions.

Table 2.1 indicates the sources of compensation available to an accident victim under the current system in a tort state, depending on the victim's insurance status, whether another driver was at least partially at fault for the accident,[9] and, if so, whether that driver was insured. The corresponding table for an add-on state[10] in which PIP coverage was available, instead of or in addition to MP coverage, would look exactly the same except that insured accident victims (those in the bottom row) would have access to PIP, if they had purchased that coverage. The corresponding table for a no-fault state would look exactly the same except that insured accident victims (those in the bottom row) would have access to PIP in every case.

Table 2.1

Compensation Sources for Accident Victims Under the Current System

Insurance Status	Other Driver at Least Partially at Fault		No Other Driver at Fault
	Uninsured	Insured	
Uninsured victim	0	BI	0
Insured victim	UM	MP + BI	MP

To estimate compensation costs for each state, we use our data on the compensation given to a representative sample of accident victims and the associated transaction costs, as follows.

---

[9]In our earlier studies, we assumed that all victims injured in multicar accidents had access to another driver's third-party coverage with the probability that the other driver was insured. In this study, we assume that victims who were injured in accidents in which no other driver was at least partially at fault have access only to their own first-party coverage, regardless of the number of cars involved in the accident. Specifically, we assume, using IRC data, that 30 percent of victims were injured in accidents in which no other driver was at least partially at fault. Section 3 presents tests of the sensitivity of the results to alternative assumptions regarding the percentage.

[10]Add-on states are those in which PIP coverage is available, but there is no tort threshold.

Uninsured Accident Victims

We assume that an uninsured accident victim injured either in an accident caused by a driver who is also uninsured or in an accident in which no other driver is at least partially at fault receives no compensation from auto insurance.

We estimate the costs of compensating an uninsured accident victim injured in an accident with an insured at-fault driver as the average compensation paid on BI claims times the probability that an accident victim exceeds the tort threshold.[11] We assume that average transaction costs are 18 percent of BI compensation in all states.

Insured Accident Victims

We estimate the costs in tort states of compensating an insured accident victim injured in an accident caused by an uninsured driver as the average compensation paid on UM claims times the fraction of insured drivers in the state who purchased UM coverage (0.89).[12]

In the no-fault states, we assume compensation costs as the average compensation paid on PIP claims, plus the average compensation paid on UM claims, times the fraction of insured drivers in the state who purchased UM coverage, times the probability that an accident victim exceeds the tort threshold. We assume that average transaction costs are 9 percent of PIP compensation paid and 18 percent of UM compensation paid.

We estimate the costs of compensating an insured accident victim injured in an accident with another insured driver in a tort (no-fault) state as the sum of the average compensation paid on BI claims in that state plus transaction costs, plus the average compensation paid on MP (PIP) claims in that state plus transaction costs, times the probability that the victim will claim against both his or her own first-party and the other driver's third-party coverages. We use the ratio of MP-earned exposures to BI-earned exposures in each state as our estimate of the fraction of insured accident victims who have access to MP coverage.[13]

---

[11]By definition, all accident victims "exceed the tort threshold" in tort states. In a no-fault state, we take the fraction of PIP claims that the claims adjuster judged qualified for a BI tort recovery under the no-fault law, whether or not the victim actually pursued a tort claim.

[12]We use the ratio of UM-earned exposures to BI-earned exposures in each state as our estimate of the fraction of insured accident victims who have UM coverage. The National Association of Independent Insurers (1998) reports earned exposures by coverage for all states except Massachusetts, North Carolina, South Carolina, and Texas. We use the national average ratio of exposures for these four states.

[13]National Association of Independent Insurers (1998).

We assume that all insured accident victims in the no-fault states have PIP coverage and will seek compensation under that coverage. We assume that transaction costs are 9 percent of MP or PIP compensation paid and 18 percent of BI compensation paid.

We estimate the costs of compensating an insured accident victim injured in an accident in which no other driver was at fault in tort (no-fault) states as the average compensation paid on MP (PIP) claims times the fraction of insured drivers in the state who purchased MP (PIP) coverage. We assume that transaction costs are 9 percent of MP or PIP compensation paid.

Estimating the Distribution of Accident Victims

Because state-specific estimates of uninsured-motorist rates are not readily available, we take a parametric approach: We assume that the uninsured-motorist rate is 15 percent.[14] We then compute the resulting fraction of accident victims that would be found in each cell of Table 2.1, multiply that fraction by the corresponding compensation costs, and sum over the cells. The result is an estimate of the average cost of compensating an accident victim in each state under that state's current system. The product of this estimate and the ratio of accident victims to insured drivers in that state is the amount that the state's insured drivers would have to be charged, on average, to recover the costs of compensating all victims. We then vary the assumed uninsured-motorist rate and repeat the procedure. Section 3 describes the sensitivity of the results to the assumed uninsured-motorist rate.

Note that under the assumption that insurance purchase decisions are statistically independent of subsequent accidents and the resulting injuries and losses, the estimates we obtain for each state are identical to those we would have obtained by estimating expected compensation outcomes for each individual victim and averaging over the victims in the sample for each state. In other words, the method outlined above essentially takes account of the variations in relevant accident characteristics (e.g., the victim's negligence) and injuries/losses among individual accident victims.

---

[14]Using the ratio of UM to BI claim frequencies to estimate the uninsured-motorist rate, the Insurance Research Council (1999) estimates that, on average, about 14 percent of drivers are uninsured. Miller, Rapp, Herbers, & Terry, Inc., an actuarial consulting firm, estimated the frequencies of UM and BI claims in the tort states in the early 1990s. The ratio of their estimates is about 0.15 (private communication).

Estimating Compensation Costs Under the Choice System

To estimate average compensation costs under the choice system, we made assumptions about drivers' insurance purchase decisions and estimated what insurers' compensation costs will be given those assumptions. In Section 3, we explore the sensitivity of our results to these assumptions and provide estimates of what costs would be under alternative assumptions.

Observe a driver who is uninsured under his or her state's current system and has declined to purchase the coverage—BI or no-fault—mandated under that system. We assume that, under choice, that driver would *not* purchase the coverage that he or she declined before ANF became an option. Thus, under choice, a driver who is uninsured in the current system would either remain uninsured or would opt for ANF under the choice plan. Similarly, a driver who is insured under his or her state's current system preferred the coverage—BI or no-fault—mandated under that system to going uninsured. Hence, we assume that if a driver *does* have insurance under his or her state's current system, he or she would elect either to retain the modified version of that insurance or to switch to ANF under choice, but would *not* decide to drop automobile insurance coverage altogether.

Given these assumptions, Table 2.2 indicates the sources of compensation available to accident victims in a tort state under the choice plan, depending on their insurance status, whether another driver was at least partially responsible for the accident, and, if so, whether the other driver involved in the accident was insured. The corresponding table for a no-fault state would look exactly the

Table 2.2

Compensation Sources for Accident Victims Under the Choice System

Insurance Status	Other Driver at Least Partially at Fault			No Other Driver at Fault
	Uninsured	ANF	MCS	
Uninsured victim	0	XEL[a]	BI	0
ANF victim	PPI	PPI + XEL	PPI + XEL	PPI
MCS victim	UM	TM + XEL	MP + BI	MP

[a]XEL denotes excess economic loss.

same except that insured accident victims (those in the bottom row) would have access to PIP in every case.

In each state, we estimate compensation costs under the choice plan as follows.

Accidents Not Involving an ANF Insured

The current system's compensation rules govern in accidents that do not involve a victim or driver covered by ANF under choice. We use the methods described above to estimate compensation in these cases.

Uninsured Victims of Accidents Caused by an ANF Insured

An uninsured victim injured in an accident involving another car whose driver switched to ANF is compensated by the other driver's supplemental BI insurance for any economic loss in excess of the mandated PPI policy limit. We estimate the expected value of compensation for excess economic loss, denoted XEL in Table 2.2, in three steps: First, we compute the difference, if positive, between the victim's economic loss and the mandated PPI limit up to each possible value of the BI policy limit, weighted by the distribution of BI policy limits in the state. We then multiply by one minus the victim's degree of fault for the accident. Finally, we average over all victims in the state. We assume that transaction costs are 49 percent of compensation paid for excess economic loss—18 percent in insurer's costs and 31 percent in plaintiff's attorney fees.[15]

Accident Victims Covered by ANF

We estimate compensation costs for accident victims covered by ANF under choice as their own PPI coverage plus recovery of excess economic loss. We estimate PPI as the average value of victims' economic losses up to the PPI policy limit. We estimate XEL as described above. We assume that transaction costs are 9 percent of PPI compensation and 49 percent of XEL compensation.

Victims Covered by the Modified Current System Injured in Accidents Caused by an ANF Insured

Victims covered by MCS who are injured in an accident caused by a driver who switched to ANF are compensated by their own TM coverage. Because the amount an accident victim can recover under TM is governed by the same rules that govern the amount an insured driver can recover under the state's current system, we estimate average TM compensation costs using the methods

---

[15]Because the plan provides that victims who seek recovery of excess economic losses may recover their legal costs, we assume that all such victims will seek representation.

described above to estimate BI compensation costs under the current system. Drivers who chose MCS are compensated by the other driver's supplemental BI insurance for any economic loss in excess of the TM policy limit. We estimate XEL for victims covered by MCS as the difference, if positive, between the victim's economic loss and his or her TM recovery up to each possible value of the BI policy limit, weighted by the distribution of BI policy limits in the state. We then multiply by one minus the victim's degree of fault for the accident. Finally, we average over all victims in the state. We assume that transaction costs are 18 percent of TM compensation paid and 49 percent of XEL compensation.

Given the assumed uninsured motorist rate under the current system and the other parameters that describe claiming patterns under the current system, the distribution of accident victims among the cells in Table 2.2 depends on the rate at which drivers who would have been insured under the current system opt for ANF coverage and the rate at which drivers who would have gone uninsured under the current system opt for ANF coverage. We have no data that allow us to estimate what either of these rates would be in any particular state. Accordingly, we take a parametric approach: We assume values for each of these rates, estimate the effects of the choice plan conditional on those values, and then revise the assumed values and repeat the analysis.

We assume that drivers' insurance purchase decisions are statistically independent of whether or not they will cause, or be injured in, an auto accident. We group drivers into three types according to their insurance purchase decisions and estimate the compensation costs insurers incur on behalf of each type of driver. Specifically, we estimate the costs incurred by insurers under policies purchased by the following:

- *Stayers*—drivers insured under the current system who would select MCS under choice.

- *Insured switchers*—drivers insured under the current system who would select ANF under choice.

- *Uninsured switchers*—drivers uninsured under the current system who would select ANF under choice.

We used the methods discussed above to compute the probability that an accident victim would fall into each cell in Table 2.2. We then multiplied those probabilities by the corresponding compensation costs. The result is an estimate of the average costs insurers incur in compensating a representative sample of accident victims in each state under the choice plan on behalf of drivers who make each possible type of insurance purchase decision. In any state, the estimate for each type of driver, multiplied by the ratio of accident victims paid on behalf of that type of driver to the number of insured drivers of that type, is the average amount insurers would have to charge that type of driver to recover the costs of compensating victims on their behalf. (Recall that we lack data on the number of accident victims per insured driver of each type in each state. As noted above, this number will cancel out when we compute the ratio of compensation costs under the current system to compensation costs under the choice plan for each type of driver.)

Note that, under the assumption that insurance purchase decisions are statistically independent of subsequent accidents and the resulting injuries/losses, the estimates we obtain for each state are identical to those we would have obtained by estimating expected compensation outcomes for each individual victim and averaging over the victims in the sample for each state. In other words, the method outlined above essentially takes account of the variations in relevant accident characteristics (e.g., the victim's negligence) and injuries and losses among individual accident victims.

Break-Even Personal Injury Premiums

To calculate the break-even personal injury premium for the current system, assume that there are N drivers, that the average driver is involved in k injury-producing accidents per year, and that each injury costs insurers C dollars, on average, including transaction costs (that is, C dollars for *every* injury, including injuries suffered by pedestrians, passengers, bicyclists, and insured and uninsured drivers). Insurers will pay out kNC dollars a year.

Let X denote the fraction of all drivers who are insured. Let P be the average premium that insurers must charge to just cover what they pay out in claims and associated transaction costs. To break even, P must be set such that XNP = kNC. Thus, the break-even premium is P = kC/X. We know how to calculate C. In calculating relative savings under choice, we will assume the value of X and specify k as an unknown parameter.

Relative Savings on Compensation Costs

To calculate *relative* savings on compensation costs, we extended the above notation to three notional insurance companies. The first sells all the insurance policies purchased by drivers in a state under its current system. The second sells all insurance policies purchased by drivers in that state who elect MCS under the choice plan. The third sells all insurance policies purchased by drivers in that state who elect ANF under the choice plan. The effects of the choice plan on the costs insurers incur on behalf of drivers who are insured in the traditional system and who would elect MCS under choice are reflected in the ratio of the second company's break-even premium to the first company's break-even premium. Similarly, the effects of the choice plan on the costs insurers incur on behalf of drivers who are insured in the current system and who would elect ANF under choice are reflected in the ratio of the third and first companies' break-even premiums.

Assume that the fraction of drivers insured in the current system is X_1 and that the company that insures them pays out an average C_1 dollars for every injury. The corresponding parameters for the company that insures drivers electing MCS under choice are X_c and C_c, respectively. The break-even personal injury premium for the current system company is $P_1 = kC_1/X_1$. The break-even personal injury premium for the company that insures MCS electors under choice is $P_c = kC_c/X_c$. The ratio of the two companies' break-even personal injury premiums is P_c/P_1. The number of injury-producing accidents per driver per year, k, cancels out, and this expression depends only on the fraction insured by each company (X) and the amount of compensation paid for each injury (C).

In our calculations, we made assumptions about X and estimated C. Thus, without knowing the accident rate but assuming that it remains the same, we could compare the relative change in the break-even personal injury premium for drivers who elect their state's MCS or ANF under choice.

Relative Savings on Total Premiums

The calculations described above yield estimates of the average compensation costs insurers will incur on behalf of stayers, insured switchers, and uninsured switchers under choice, relative to the compensation costs they would have incurred on behalf of each type of driver under their state's current system. Insurers' other expenses include commissions and other selling expenses, general expenses, state premium taxes, licenses and fees, and dividends to policyholders. NAIC (1997) provides state-specific estimates of claims costs and other expenses for liability claims. The relationship between claims costs and other expenses for liability claims is highly linear and essentially goes through the origin. The R squared for a regression of insurers' other expenses on claims costs is 0.97; the intercept is indistinguishable from zero. If insurers' other expenses include any fixed costs, those costs are sufficiently small relative to the variable component of other expenses that other expenses are essentially proportional to claims costs.

We assume that insurers' profit margins on MCS insureds will be the same as on ANF insureds and that the return on investment income is independent of the mix of insureds.

To translate the effects on compensation costs under personal injury coverages into effects on total auto insurance premiums, we multiply our estimate of compensation cost savings by the proportion of total auto insurance premiums in each state that were spent for personal injury coverages in 1997, the most recent year for which data are available.

3. Results and Sensitivity Analysis

Overview

We have no data that allow us to estimate the fraction of drivers in each state who would purchase insurance under the current system and the fraction that would switch to ANF under choice. We consider a base case in which we assume that 50 percent of currently insured drivers switch to ANF. We also consider the case in which all currently insured drivers elect ANF under choice. The savings realized by currently insured drivers who elect ANF under choice do not depend on the percentage of uninsured drivers who elect ANF under choice. Table 3.1 summarizes the results of the analysis.

We estimate that if half the insured drivers in the *tort states* were to switch to ANF under the choice plan, the costs of compensating victims on their behalf would be reduced about 54 percent from what they would have been had those drivers been insured under the traditional tort system. If insurers' other costs vary in proportion to compensation costs, this would translate into a 22 percent reduction in total auto insurance premiums. Adoption of the choice plan would have little effect on the costs of compensating victims on behalf of drivers who choose to stay under the modified version of the current system.

Averaging over the *no-fault states*, we find that if half the insured drivers were to switch to ANF under the choice plan, the costs of compensating victims on their behalf would be reduced about 63 percent from what the costs would have been

Table 3.1

Relative Savings for Previously Insured Drivers
(in percent)

Scenario	Insurance Class	Premium	Relative Savings		
			Tort States	No-Fault States	All States
Half switch	Switchers	Personal injury	54	63	57
		Total	22	29	24
	Stayers	Personal injury	7	15	10
		Total	3	7	4
All switch	Switchers	Personal injury	51	63	56
		Total	21	29	23

had those drivers been insured under their state's current system. If insurers' other costs vary in proportion to compensation costs, this would translate into a 29 percent reduction in total auto insurance premiums. Adoption of the choice plan would reduce the costs of compensating victims on behalf of drivers who elect to remain in the modified current system by about 15 percent, resulting in a 7 percent savings on their total premiums.

Averaging over *all states combined,* we find that compensation costs incurred on behalf of insured switchers would be reduced about 57 percent. This translates into about a 24 percent reduction in total premiums.

Assuming that all insured drivers switch to ANF has little effect on the estimates. In the tort states, compensation costs would be reduced about 51 percent, which translates into a 21 percent reduction in total auto insurance premiums. The corresponding estimates for the no-fault states are a 63 percent reduction in compensation costs and a 29 percent reduction in total auto insurance premiums. For all states combined, compensation costs incurred on behalf of insured switchers would be reduced about 56 percent. This translates into about a 24 percent reduction in total premiums.

In both the tort states and the no-fault states, differences among states are relatively small. Whatever differences there are may reflect sampling variation in the data or differences in the extent to which our assumptions apply. In any case, our general results are robust with respect to interstate variations in the distributions of accidents and injuries. This suggests that, even if these distributions vary over time in any state, the variations are not likely to significantly affect our results.

The Effects of the Choice Plan on Costs

Tables 3.2 and 3.3 present state-by-state estimates[1] of the average percentage reduction in both personal injury compensation costs and total auto insurance premiums that policyholders who elect either their state's MCS or ANF would realize in each of the states. These estimates assume that

- 15 percent of drivers in the state were uninsured under the current system,
- either 50 percent or 100 percent of the drivers insured under the current system would opt for ANF if given the choice, and

---

[1] We report the effects of the choice plan on Pennsylvania drivers covered by tort in 1997 in Table 3.2. We report the effects of the choice plan on Pennsylvania drivers covered by the verbal threshold no-fault plan in 1997 in Table 3.3.

- half of all drivers who were uninsured under the current system would opt for ANF if given the choice.

Table 3.2

Relative Savings Under Choice by State: Tort States
(in percent)

| | Half Switch Scenario | | | | All Switch Scenario | |
| | Switchers | | Stayers | | Switchers | |
State	Injury Premium	Total Premium	Injury Premium	Total Premium	Injury Premium	Total Premium
Alabama	53	17	6	2	50	16
Alaska	65	26	13	5	66	26
Arizona	51	23	7	3	49	23
Arkansas	57	20	9	3	57	20
California	47	22	6	3	45	21
Connecticut	62	28	7	3	61	28
Delaware	61	31	9	5	55	28
Georgia	52	18	5	2	49	17
Idaho	54	21	0	0	54	21
Illinois	56	20	8	3	52	19
Indiana	58	22	6	2	55	21
Iowa	55	20	6	2	53	19
Louisiana	72	34	13	6	70	33
Maine	65	25	10	4	63	24
Maryland	55	23	7	3	54	23
Mississippi	49	17	5	2	46	15
Missouri	54	19	8	3	52	19
Montana	47	18	3	1	42	16
Nebraska	49	17	1	0	48	16
Nevada	54	28	7	3	51	26
New Hampshire	52	20	7	3	49	19
New Mexico	50	23	9	4	51	23
North Carolina	47	19	6	2	45	18
Ohio	61	24	7	3	58	23
Oklahoma	49	19	7	3	48	19
Oregon	51	22	6	3	50	22
Penn (tort)	54	23	8	3	48	21
Rhode Island	70	35	18	9	70	35
South Carolina	56	23	7	3	54	22
South Dakota	60	24	10	4	60	24
Tennessee	49	17	6	2	47	16
Texas	45	22	6	3	45	22
Vermont	63	22	9	3	63	22
Virginia	52	23	8	3	50	22
Washington	55	27	6	3	54	26
West Virginia	62	28	6	3	61	27
Wisconsin	57	22	7	3	55	21
Wyoming	63	21	5	2	59	19
All tort states	54	22	7	3	51	21

Table 3.3

Relative Savings Under Choice by State: No-Fault States
(in percent)

| | Half Switch Scenario | | | | All Switch Scenario | |
| | Switchers | | Stayers | | Switchers | |
State	Injury Premium	Total Premium	Injury Premium	Total Premium	Injury Premium	Total Premium
Colorado	70	41	11	7	69	40
Florida	61	29	16	8	61	28
Kansas	76	23	14	4	74	23
Kentucky	67	28	15	7	66	28
Massachusetts	65	33	13	7	65	33
Michigan	42	15	20	7	44	15
Minnesota	63	29	13	6	62	29
New York	70	32	16	7	71	32
North Dakota	58	18	21	7	57	18
Penn (nof)	82	36	11	5	82	36
Utah	62	25	12	5	61	25
All no-fault states	63	29	16	7	63	29

Drivers who opt for ANF under choice are not liable for others' noneconomic losses. In the tort states, the compensation costs that insurers would incur on behalf of such drivers would be substantially lower than they would have been under the tort system. On the other hand, the amounts paid to them under their PPI coverages generally exceed what would be paid to them under MP insurance. In general, the savings obtained by eliminating compensation payments on their behalf for noneconomic loss under choice greatly outweigh the additional costs incurred in providing them with more-generous first-party no-fault compensation—PPI versus MP. Hence, the cost of compensating for personal injuries incurred or caused by tort state drivers who elect ANF would drop substantially—40 percent or more—relative to the costs incurred on their behalf under the traditional tort system. If insurers' other costs declined in proportion, the total premiums charged drivers who would be insured under the traditional tort system and would opt for ANF under choice would be reduced by at least 15 percent in each of the tort states.

The savings that would be realized by insured drivers who switch to ANF under choice are not very sensitive to the fraction of insured drivers who exercise that option. In most states, the savings available to an individual consumer who switches from the current system to ANF are slightly greater if half of those who would have been insured under the current system switch to ANF than if all of those who would have been insured under the current system switch to ANF. This result stems from the provision that ANF electors are liable to anyone they injure (to the degree they are responsible for that injury) for excess economic loss.

Under the plan examined here, we assume that ANF electors purchase the mandated PPI policy limit. Thus, an ANF-insured driver who injures someone else covered by ANF is liable for the victim's economic losses in excess of the PPI policy limit. An ANF-insured driver who injures someone covered by MCS is liable for the victim's economic losses in excess of his or her TM policy limit. We assume that the distribution of TM policy limits purchased by consumers who elect the modified current system under choice is the same as the distribution of BI policy limits purchased by consumers under the current system. Because BI limits are at least as large as the mandated PPI limit and sometimes larger, the expected excess economic losses incurred by victims who are covered by TM are less, on average, than the expected excess economic losses incurred by victims covered by PPI.

A driver who elected MCS and is involved in an accident with a driver who chose ANF is entirely free from liability to the other driver for noneconomic loss; his insurer would pay out less, on average, under choice than under the current system. But a driver who chose MCS and is injured in an accident with a driver who chose ANF must turn to his own TM coverage, rather than to the other driver, for recovery of his own noneconomic loss. His insurer saves the costs of compensating the other driver for noneconomic loss but incurs the additional costs of compensating the insured for his own noneconomic loss. If there is no adverse selection in the choices made under the choice plan, drivers who choose MCS will have the same average noneconomic loss and negligence as do drivers who elect ANF, and these savings will approximately equal the additional costs.

Current no-fault plans already limit accident victims' access to compensation for noneconomic loss. Hence, the savings on compensation costs obtained by totally eliminating compensation payments for noneconomic loss on behalf of drivers who elect ANF in the current no-fault states are smaller than would be realized in tort states. But current no-fault plans already include PIP compensation, so no new compensation costs are incurred on behalf of drivers who elected ANF under choice in the no-fault states. Hence, compensation costs incurred on behalf of ANF electors in the no-fault states would also generally substantially decline relative to the costs incurred on their behalf under their state's current system. On average, the cost of compensating for personal injuries incurred or caused by insured drivers in the no-fault states who elected ANF would drop more than 60 percent in most states—relative to the costs incurred on their behalf under the current no-fault system. If insurers' other costs declined in proportion, the total premiums charged drivers who would be insured under the current system and would opt for ANF under choice would be reduced by about 27 percent in most no-fault states.

24

The savings that would be realized by insured drivers who switch to ANF under choice are not very sensitive to the fraction of insured drivers who exercise that option. The estimated savings to drivers when 50 percent of insured drivers switch to ANF are very similar to the savings estimates when all insured drivers switch to ANF.

As in the tort states, drivers who elected MCS and are involved in an accident with a driver who chose ANF are entirely free from liability to the other driver for noneconomic loss; their insurers would pay out less, on average, under choice than under the current system. But drivers who chose MCS and are injured in an accident with a driver who chose ANF must turn to their own TM coverage for recovery of their own noneconomic losses. Their insurers save the costs of compensating the other driver for noneconomic loss but incur the additional costs of compensating the insured for his own noneconomic loss. If there is no adverse selection in the choices made under the choice plan, drivers who choose MCS will have the same average noneconomic loss and negligence as do drivers who elect ANF, and these savings will approximately equal the additional costs.

The Effects of the Choice Plan on Compensation

Figure 3.1 draws on the results for California to illustrate the effects of the choice plan on compensation outcomes. These results are for a scenario in which 50

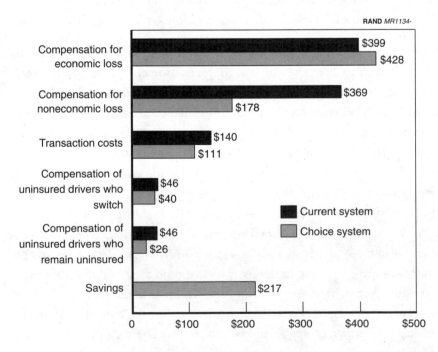

Figure 3.1—Effects of Choice Plan on Compensation Outcomes in California

percent of insured and 50 percent of uninsured drivers elect ANF under choice. The dark bars illustrate how $1,000 in compensation costs would be distributed in California under the current system. The dollar figure attached to each bar shows the amount that would be spent on that cost category. The light bars illustrate how these compensation costs would be affected by the choice plan, assuming the base-case insurance parameters. The dollar figure attached to each of the light bars shows the amount that would be spent in each cost category under the choice system.

For purposes of this comparison, we count all money paid to accident victims as compensation for economic loss until they have been fully compensated; we include only amounts paid to victims in excess of their economic losses as compensation for noneconomic loss. The compensation figures are gross in that they show the amount paid to accident victims in compensation without regard to any legal fees or costs that must be paid out of this amount. We distinguish between drivers who would be insured under the current system and those who would go uninsured under the current system. We divide the latter into two subgroups: those who stay uninsured under choice and those who elect to purchase ANF when it is available to them. (Because this illustration assumes that half of the uninsured drivers under the current system would switch to ANF under choice, these subgroups are equal in size.)

We estimate that if half of the insured drivers in California switched to ANF under choice, the amount paid to insured accident victims, including both those covered by ANF and those covered by MCS, for economic loss would be increased about 7 percent, on average. Out of each $1,000 spent in the current system, about $399 would be paid in compensation for economic loss to victims who have purchased insurance. Under choice, the amount of compensation paid to these victims for economic loss would be 11 percent greater, about $428. There are some differences from one victim to another in how the compensation paid to them for economic loss under the choice plan would compare with the compensation they would each have received under the current system.

About $369 out of each $1,000 spent in the current system would be paid to insured victims in compensation for noneconomic loss. Under choice, the amount of compensation paid to these victims for noneconomic loss would be cut to the extent that drivers switch to ANF. Drivers who elect MCS under choice would receive essentially the same compensation for noneconomic loss as under the current system, assuming no change in policy limits. Those who switch to ANF would receive no compensation for noneconomic loss. In the example, we assume that half the insured drivers under the current system elect MCS and half switch to ANF. Consequently, the amount paid to insured victims in compensation for noneconomic loss is reduced about half, to about $178 out of each $1,000 in compensation costs, under choice.

Insurers' transaction costs—defense fees and allocated loss adjustment expenses—account for about $140 out of each $1,000 under the current system. These costs would be cut about 15 percent, to about $111 out of each $1,000, under the choice plan for these assumed parameters. Note that the choice plan provides legal fees to ANF drivers who seek compensation for economic losses in excess of their PIP policy limits. Because this provision allows victims representation at no cost to themselves, we assume that victims will generally secure representation, even on small claims, increasing insurers' transaction costs for these claims.

The costs of compensating uninsured motorists under the current system account for $92 out of each $1,000 auto insurers spend on compensation in California. The choice plan would cut these costs about 28 percent. Uninsured drivers under the current system who switch to ANF under choice waive compensation for noneconomic loss in return for being assured compensation for economic loss. Uninsured switchers who would have gone uncompensated under the current system (e.g., an uninsured driver injured in a single-car accident) do better: They receive compensation for their economic loss. Uninsured switchers who would have obtained compensation from another driver's BI coverage for both their economic and noneconomic loss do worse. The net result is a 12 percent reduction in the compensation paid to these victims, on average. The compensation paid to drivers who remain uninsured under choice is cut to 56 percent, on average, of what it would have been under the current system. Uninsured drivers under choice who are injured in an accident with someone who opted for MCS under choice receive the same compensation they would have received under the current system. But uninsured drivers under choice who are injured in an accident with someone who opted for ANF under choice are compensated only for economic loss in excess of the mandated PPI policy limit.

The effects of the plan on compensation outcomes generally follow the pattern described above for California.

Sensitivity Analyses

Sensitivity to Assumed Parameters

The estimates presented above are for a base case in which we assume that

- 30 percent of accidents were the injured person's own fault (percent own-fault),

- 50 percent of insured accident victims who were injured by another insured driver and who have purchased MP collect from both the at-fault other driver and from their own MP policy (percent claim-both), and

- 15 percent of drivers are uninsured under the current system (percent uninsured).

To examine the sensitivity of our estimates to these parameters, we replicated the analysis for every combination of the following alternative assumptions:

- The percentage of own-fault accidents is 15, 30, or 60 percent.

- The percentage of claim-both victims is 25, 50, or 100 percent.

- The percentage of uninsured motorists before choice is 10, 15, or 20 percent.

Further, in each state, we generally find a few large settlements along with a large number of smaller ones. We reestimated the effects of the plan on insured switchers' compensation costs under each of the above 27 combinations of assumptions, assuming, in every state and for each compensation element, the following:

- The compensation provided in each of the largest 10 percent of all cases is double the actual value.

- The compensation provided in all cases, including the largest 10 percent of all cases, is the actual value.

- The compensation provided in each of the largest 10 percent of all cases is half the actual value.

In all, we developed 81 estimates of the effects of the choice plan on insured switchers' total auto insurance premiums in each state. Figure 3.2 shows the smallest, base-case, and largest of these estimates for each state, assuming that 50 percent of insured drivers elect ANF under choice. The left end of the bar shown for each state is the lowest estimate we obtained for that state. The right end is the highest estimate we obtained for that state. The line inside the bar shows the

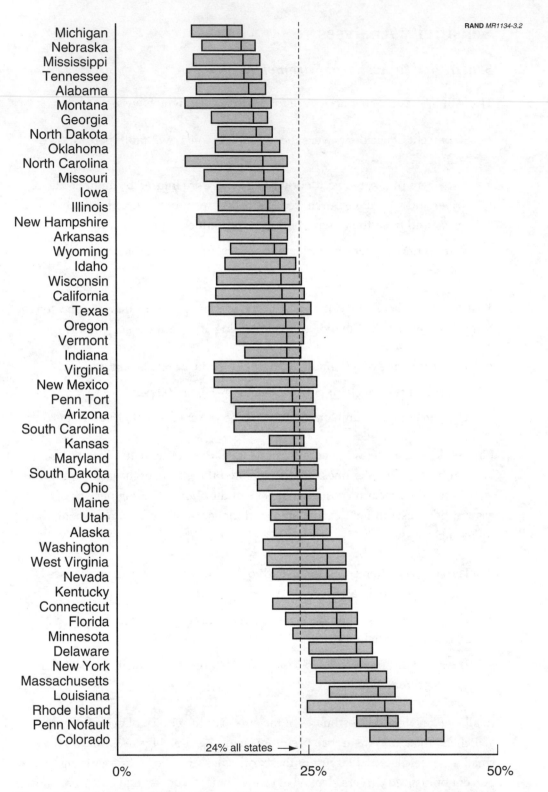

RAND *MR1134-3.2*

Figure 3.2—Relative Savings for Drivers Who Switch If Half of Insured Drivers Switch
to ANF: Smallest, Base-Case, and Largest Percentage Savings

base-case estimate for that state. The corresponding figure for the scenario in which *all* insured drivers elect ANF under choice is virtually the same.

For most states, the range of estimates is relatively small. Nothing in these estimates affects our main finding that the personal injury coverage costs of insuring drivers who elect ANF under choice will fall about 55 percent, which translates into savings of about 23 percent on their total premiums.

We used the same approach to develop 81 estimates of the effects of the choice plan on total auto insurance premiums for drivers who elect MCS in each state. Figure 3.3 shows the smallest, base-case,[2] and largest of these estimates for each state, assuming that 50 percent of insured drivers elect ANF under choice.

Here, too, the range of estimates is relatively small in most states. Nothing in these estimates affects our main finding that insured drivers who elect their state's MCS under choice will not be noticeably affected by the availability of ANF.

Sensitivity to Other Assumptions

We assumed that insurance purchase decisions are statistically independent of subsequent accidents and the resulting injuries/losses. That is, we assume that bad drivers elect either MCS or ANF with the same probabilities as do good drivers. This is consistent with the available evidence in the three states that have adopted choice plans. There is no evidence that either particularly bad or particularly good drivers in any of these states self-select into one plan or the other.

For that matter, the available evidence suggests that drivers may not have a clear understanding of their own relative driving performance. A national survey of people who suffered accidental injuries found that auto accident victims attributed their injuries to someone else more than 90 percent of the time and that even drivers injured when their vehicle struck another vehicle named themselves as the cause of the accident only 16 percent of the time.[3] If drivers did not perceive themselves as having caused an accident in which they were injured, how likely is it that these same drivers would have labeled themselves before the fact as a driver likely to be involved in an accident? Self-selection cannot affect

---

[2]The base case assumes that, in the current system, 15 percent of drivers are uninsured, 30 percent of victims are injured in accidents in which no other driver is even partially at fault, and 50 percent of victims with access to both their own and another driver's auto insurance will pursue claims against both.

[3]Hensler et al. (1991), p. 143.

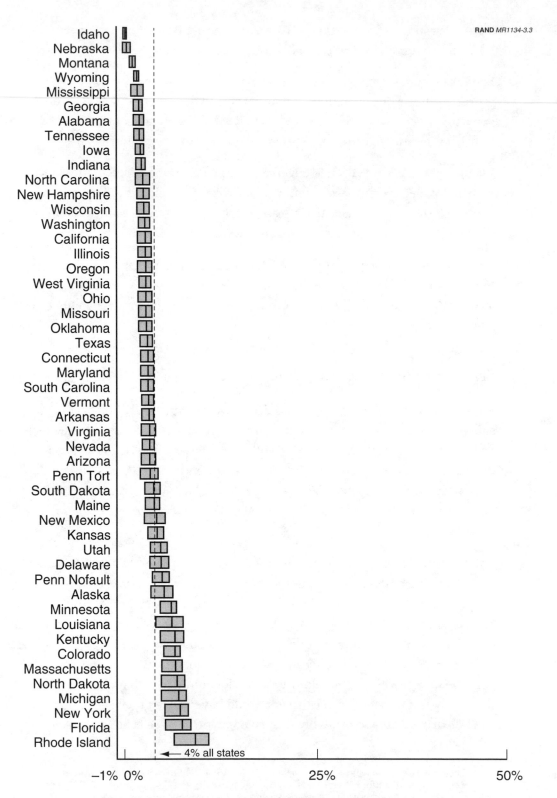

RAND MR1134-3.3

Figure 3.3—Relative Savings for Drivers Who Retain a Modified Version
of the Current System If Half of Insured Drivers Switch to ANF:
Smallest, Base-Case, and Largest Percentage Savings

the distribution of drivers between plans unless drivers accurately perceive their own driving ability.

Finally, even if bad drivers—or good drivers—accurately perceived their own driving abilities, it is not clear which option they would prefer. Drivers covered by ANF who cause accidents impose costs on their insurers for their own economic losses, so insurers have the same incentives to experience-rate drivers who elect ANF under choice as they do to experience-rate drivers who elect MCS. Similarly, "accident-prone" drivers have to consider the trade-off between the risk that the compensation available to them under MCS will be reduced to the degree that they are responsible for an accident in which they are injured and the loss of access to compensation for noneconomic loss if they elect ANF under choice.

Adverse selection is an empirical issue that warrants further study. However, the evidence now available offers no reason to suspect that adverse selection would be sufficient to dramatically affect the results.

How the 1997 Results Compare to the 1992 and 1987 Results

Our updated estimates of the savings under the choice plan generally fall between estimates based on the 1987 data and those based on the 1992 data. In most states, our estimates of the savings that would accrue to drivers who opted for ANF based on the 1992 data were lower than the corresponding estimates we had obtained using the 1987 data. These patterns generally reversed themselves, though not in every case, between 1992 and 1997. In most states, our estimates of the savings that would accrue to drivers who opted for ANF based on the 1997 data were greater than the corresponding estimate we had obtained using the 1992 data, though generally not as large as the estimates we had obtained using the 1987 data.

Table 3.4 summarizes the results we obtained using the 1987, 1992, and 1997 databases.

There are some differences among these studies in the states included in each group. Connecticut and Georgia were included in the no-fault states in the analysis of the 1987 data. Both were omitted from the analysis of the 1992 data because of data limitations; both are included in the tort states in this study. Hawaii and New Jersey were included in the no-fault states in the analysis of the 1987 data. Because of data limitations, both were omitted from the analyses of the 1992 data and the 1997 data. Pennsylvania was included in the tort states in

Table 3.4

Estimated Relative Savings for Previously Insured Drivers Based on the 1987, 1992, and 1997 Databases

Insurance System	Scenario	Insurance Class	Premium	Relative Savings (%) 1987	1992	1997
	Half switch	Switchers	Personal injury	66	46	54
			Total	31	20	22
Tort states		Stayers	Personal injury	0	1	7
			Total	0	1	3
	All switch	Switchers	Personal injury	65	44	51
			Total	30	19	21
	Half switch	Switchers	Personal injury	59	45	63
			Total	28	22	29
No-fault states		Stayers	Personal injury	0	9	15
			Total	0	4	7
	All switch	Switchers	Personal injury	59	47	63
			Total	29	23	29
	Half switch	Switchers	Personal injury	63	45	57
			Total	30	21	24
All states		Stayers	Personal injury	0	5	10
			Total	0	2	4
	All switch	Switchers	Personal injury	62	45	55
			Total	30	20	23

the 1987 data analysis. The results for Pennsylvania drivers who elected the limited no-fault (tort) option under Pennsylvania's choice plan are included in the no-fault (tort) results in the analyses of the 1992 and the 1997 data.

We believe that changes in the savings estimates are largely due to changes in the average economic losses claimed by accident victims. An accident victim covered by ANF would be compensated for economic loss regardless of fault. Because victims injured in accidents in which no other driver was at fault frequently receive less than full compensation for their economic losses under the current system, many of these victims would be more fully compensated, at greater expense to the insurance system, under ANF. Thus, increases in economic losses increase the expected costs incurred on behalf of those who switch to ANF under choice. At the same time, an ANF-insured victim injured by another driver does not receive the compensation for noneconomic loss that would be provided him or her under the current system. But the amount of compensation for noneconomic loss available to a victim is generally limited to the difference between the injuring driver's BI policy limit and the victim's economic loss. Because drivers tend not to increase their policy limits over time, increases in economic loss squeeze compensation for noneconomic loss and reduce the extent to which ANF provides savings relative to the current system.

The victims in the 1992 database claimed economic losses that were much greater, on average, than the losses claimed by the victims in the 1987 database. Hence, the estimated savings attendant on electing ANF were smaller in most states in 1992 than they had been in 1987. Conversely, average claimed economic losses actually declined in about half of the states between 1992 and 1997. In these states, the reduction in claimed economic loss generally led to increased savings for those who elected ANF.

4. Conclusions

Because we focus on the financial implications of the choice plan, our work does not address the degree to which accident victims derive satisfaction from being compensated under an insurance policy purchased by the driver who injured them.[1] Nor do we consider the satisfaction that consumers who value access to compensation for noneconomic loss derive from being able to determine for themselves the limits on what they can obtain if injured by another driver in an auto accident rather than facing the uncertainty of the policy limit purchased by that driver.

Our results, however, do suggest that the choice plan can deliver on its promise to offer dramatically less expensive insurance to drivers willing to give up access to compensation for noneconomic loss, with little actual effect on those who want to retain access to compensation for both economic and noneconomic loss. If insurers pass on cost savings, the adoption of a choice plan would

- allow drivers who are willing to waive their tort rights to buy ANF personal injury coverage for roughly 56 percent of what they have to pay for personal injury coverage under their state's current system, which translates into savings on total premiums of about 23 percent on their total premiums, on average, and

- allow drivers who prefer to remain within a somewhat modified version of their state's current system to do so, at essentially the same costs as under their state's current system.

---

[1]See Hensler et al. (1991), Section V, for a review of the literature on the factors that motivate claiming.

Appendix
Technical Details

If

f = fraction no other driver at fault,

b = fraction uninsured, and

g = fraction claiming both medpay and personal injury,

then Table A.1 is the distribution of accident victims.

Table A.1

Distribution of Accident Victims

Accident Victim	Other Driver at Least Partially at Fault		No Other Driver at Fault
	Uninsured	Insured	
Uninsured	$(1-f)b^2$	$(1-f)(1-b)b$	fb
Insured	$(1-f)(1-b)b$	$(1-f)(1-b)^2$	$f(1-b)$

Now suppose that for any particular coverage (e.g., medical payments), the probability that, *if* an accident falls in cell row i, column j, of Table A.1, *then* a claim will be made under that coverage is g_{ij}. We call these g's the claiming probabilities for this form of coverage.

If the total number of accidents is A, then the total number of claims under this coverage is

$$C = A\Sigma p_{ij}g_{ij}$$

where p_{ij} is the probability displayed in row i, column j, of Table A.1.

Now suppose it is known that a total of C claims were made for a particular form of coverage. Then, of course,

$$A = C/\Sigma p_{ij}g_{ij}$$

and the number of claims under this coverage that we would see in row i, column j, of Table A.1 would be

$$C_{ij} = A p_{ij}g_{ij} = C p_{ij}g_{ij}/\Sigma p_{ij}g_{ij}. \tag{1}$$

Uninsured Motorist Claims

Only an insured accident victim involved with another driver who is at least partially at fault will make a UM claim. Therefore, all uninsured motorist claims fall into the second row, first column, of Table A.1.

Bodily Injury Claims

A BI claim can be made only if there is another driver who is at least partially at fault and is insured. Such a claim can be made regardless of the insurance status of the accident victim. Therefore, all personal injury claims fall into the two cells in the second column of Table A.1. Applying Eq. (1), the number of bodily injury claims in each cell of the matrix is given in Table A.2.

Table A.2

Distribution of BI Claims

Accident Victim	Other Driver at Least Partially at Fault		No Other Diver at Fault
	Uninsured	Insured	
Uninsured		bB	
Insured		$(1-b)B$	

where B is the number of BI claims.

Medical Payments/Personal Injury Protection

In a tort (no-fault) state, an MP (PIP) claim may be made under two different circumstances:

- The accident victim is insured and there is no other driver at fault, or

- The accident victim is insured, there is an insured other driver who is at least partially at fault (the victim's injury exceeds the threshold), and the accident victim chooses to claim under both his or her own MP (PIP) policy and the other driver's policy.

Therefore, all MP (PIP) claims fall into the cells in the second row, second and third columns, of Table A.1. Applying Eq. (1), if there are P MP (PIP) claims, the number of such claims in each cell of the matrix is given in Table A.3.

Table A.3

Distribution of MP (PIP) Claims

| Accident Victim | Other Driver at Least Partially at Fault | | No Other Driver at Fault |
	Uninsured	Insured	
Uninsured			
Insured		$(1-b)(1-f)gP/D$	fP/D

where P = number of MP/PIP claims, and D = $(1-b)(1-f)g + f$.

Distribution of Personal Injury Claims

Given a particular number of bodily injury, medical payment/personal injury protection, and uninsured motorist claims, these claims will fall into the six cells of Table A.1 according to the formulas given in Table A.4, where U is the number of UM claims.

Table A.4

Distribution of Claims Under the Current System

| Accident Victim | Other Driver at Least Partially at Fault | | No Other Driver at Fault |
	Uninsured	Insured	
Uninsured		bB	
Insured	U	$(1-b)B + (1-b)(1-f)gP/D$	fP/D

Bibliography

Abrahamse, Allan, and Stephen J. Carroll, *The Effects of a Choice Automobile Insurance Plan Under Consideration by the Joint Economic Committee of the United States Congress,* Santa Monica, CA: RAND, DRU-1609-ICJ, April 1997.

Abrahamse, Allan, and Stephen J. Carroll, *The Effects of a Choice Auto Insurance Plan on Insurance Costs,* Santa Monica, CA: RAND, MR-540-ICJ, 1995.

All-Industry Research Advisory Council, *Uninsured Motorists,* Oak Brook, IL: 1989.

Carroll, Stephen J., and Allan Abrahamse, *The Effects of a Choice Automobile Insurance Plan on Insurance Costs and Compensation: An Updated Analysis,* Santa Monica, CA: RAND, MR-970-ICJ, 1998.

Carroll, Stephen J., et al., *The Costs of Excess Medical Claims for Automobile Personal Injuries,* Santa Monica, CA: RAND, DB-139-ICJ, 1995.

Carroll, Stephen J., and James Kakalik, "No-Fault Approaches to Compensating Auto Accident Victims," *Journal of Risk and Insurance,* Vol. 60, No. 2, 1993, pp. 265–287.

Carroll, Stephen J., et al., *No-Fault Approaches to Compensating People Injured in Automobile Accidents,* Santa Monica, CA: RAND, R-4019-ICJ, 1991.

Hensler, Deborah R., et al., *Compensation for Accidental Injuries in the United States,* Santa Monica, CA: RAND, R-3999-HHS/ICJ, 1991.

Insurance Research Council, *Uninsured Motorists,* Malvern, PA, 1999a.

Insurance Research Council, *Injuries in Auto Accidents,* Malvern, PA, June 1999b.

Insurance Research Council, *Fraud and Buildup in Auto Insurance Claims,* Malvern, PA, September 1996.

National Association of Independent Insurers, *Private Passenger Automobile Experience,* Des Plaines, IL, 1998.

National Association of Insurance Commissioners, *State Average Expenditures and Premiums for Personal Automobile Insurance in 1997,* Kansas City, MO, March 1999.

National Association of Insurance Commissioners, *Profitability by Line by State in 1997,* Kansas City, MO, December 1998.

O'Connell, Jeffrey, Stephen J. Carroll, Michael Horowitz, Allan Abrahamse, and Paul Jamieson, "The Comparative Costs of Allowing Consumer Choice for Auto Insurance in All Fifty States," *Maryland Law Review,* Vol. 55, No. 1, 1996, pp. 160–222.

O'Connell, Jeffrey, Stephen J. Carroll, Michael Horowitz, Allan Abrahamse, and Daniel Kaiser, "The Costs of Consumer Choice for Auto Insurance in States Without No-Fault Insurance," *Maryland Law Review*, Vol. 54, No. 2, 1995, pp. 281–351.

O'Connell, Jeffrey, Stephen J. Carroll, Michael Horowitz, and Allan Abrahamse, "Consumer Choice in the Auto Insurance Market," *Maryland Law Review*, Vol. 52, No. 4, 1993, pp. 1016–1062.

O'Connell, Jeffrey, and Robert H. Joost, "Giving Motorists a Choice Between Fault and No-Fault Insurance," *Virginia Law Review,* Vol. 72, No. 1, 1986, pp. 61–89.